The Library of Planets™

SATURN

Charles Hofer

rosen publishing's
rosen central®

New York

Published in 2009 by The Rosen Publishing Group, Inc.
29 East 21st Street, New York, NY 10010

Revised Edition

Library of Congress Cataloging-in-Publication Data

Hofer, Charles.
Saturn / Charles Hofer.—1st ed.
        p. cm.—(The library of planets)
Includes bibliographical references and index.
ISBN-13: 978-1-4358-5075-0 (library binding)
1. Saturn (Planet)—Juvenile literature. I. Title.
QB671.H64 2008
523.46—dc22

                                                                        2008014900

Manufactured in the United States of America

On the cover: An image of Saturn and its rings taken by *Voyager 2.*

Contents

INTRODUCTION

Saturn, the sixth planet from the Sun, was the most distant planet known to ancient peoples. Since prehistoric times, Saturn has been visible with the naked eye as a slow-moving and distant light. The first people to record sightings of Saturn were the ancient Assyrians, who lived in what is now Iraq. Around 700 BCE, the Assyrians spotted this bright body in the sky and named it the Star of Ninib, in honor of the Assyrian sun god of springtime. Eventually, the culture surrounding Ninib was adopted by cultures in Greece and Rome.

Around 400 BCE, the Greeks spotted this wandering body and named it Cronus, ruler of the Titans. The Romans, who borrowed much of their culture from the Greeks, later changed the planet's name to Saturn. Both the ancient cultures of Greece and Rome identified Saturn as the original king of all gods. The Saturn/Cronus myth was filled with blood and warfare, and the stories from both Rome and Greece are quite similar.

According to the Saturn/Cronus myth, Saturn was a Titan, an ancient race of giants that ruled over the universe. Under Saturn, the

In ancient mythology, Saturn (to the Romans; Cronus to the Greeks) was the god of agriculture. He was a Titan, one of the gods who ruled the universe. But Saturn eventually turned into an evil creature, devouring his children. Shown here is a painting in which Saturn is doing just that.

world flourished during a golden age. During this golden age, society became more civilized.

But all was not well in the heavens. Saturn eventually turned into a darker being, much like nature itself, which can unleash droughts, floods, and other disasters on man. Soon, Saturn began to devour his children, one by one. Jupiter (known as Zeus in Greek mythology) was a courageous son of Saturn's and soon emerged as the leader of the other gods, who included Mars (Ares), Venus (Aphrodite), and Mercury (Hermes). These gods, led by Jupiter, plotted to overthrow the Titans and remove Saturn from the throne. When Saturn swallowed his son, Jupiter escaped by smashing through Saturn's skull.

One

A Unique Feature

From the first sightings by ancient peoples until the sixteenth century, Saturn gave only a distant glimpse of the heavens. The planet itself would stay shrouded in mystery until 1610, when an astronomer named Galileo Galilei put to work an invention he had recently improved—the telescope.

Galileo Galilei

Born in Pisa, Italy, on February 15, 1564, Galileo would become known as the founder of modern experimental science. After spending most of his childhood in Florence, Italy, Galileo began studying at the University of Pisa in 1581. While his father hoped he would study medicine, Galileo quickly became entranced with the world of science, especially mathematics.

Telescopes that existed before 1610 could magnify an object only about three times. Galileo improved on these telescopes so much that his telescope could magnify an object twenty times. Before Galileo's improvements, man's picture of space was limited to the nearby stars in the sky and what could be seen on the surface of the Moon by the naked eye. With Galileo's new and vastly improved telescope, man could now look deep into space.

With his new telescope, Galileo made many important discoveries about outer space. Some of his observations included

sunspots, four of Jupiter's moons, the cycles of Venus, and the first sighting of Saturn's fantastic rings.

Saturn: The "Tri-Form" Planet

In 1610, while he was observing Saturn through his new telescope, Galileo became rather confused. At first, he believed he was looking at three planets. To Galileo, Saturn looked as though it was one large planet with a smaller planet on each side.

Though Galileo did not invent the telescope, he improved it. Because of his improvements, he was able to see farther into space and with more detail. It can be said that the slight improvements that Galileo made to the telescope greatly improved our understanding of the universe. Shown here are some of the telescopes Galileo originally used.

He quickly dashed off a letter to a friend, the German astronomer Johannes Kepler. Galileo wrote a cryptic message in Latin: "*Altissimum planetam tergeminum observavi,*" or "I have observed the highest planet tri-form." Kepler then sent Galileo's message to the Austrian emperor, Rudolf II, who requested an explanation from Galileo. Galileo responded that Saturn was not just a single planet but three planets that touch each other. But Galileo would later be unable to prove his own theory.

Two years after his first sighting of Saturn as a "tri-form" planet, Galileo was astonished to observe that the appearance of what he thought were two smaller planets had vanished. The main body of Saturn was now all by itself. Galileo could not explain the phenomenon.

Shown here is an image of Saturn and its rings taken by the *Voyager 2* spacecraft from a distance of twenty-one million miles (thirty-four million kilometers). With Galileo's primitive telescope and knowing that he saw Saturn from Earth, where the atmosphere can obstruct the view, it is easy to understand why he mistook Saturn's rings for planets.

We now know that what he thought were other planets were simply the rings of Saturn. What Galileo saw never disappeared, as he believed they had. Since the rings of Saturn are relatively flat, Galileo was simply tricked by his own observations. Later it was learned that this "disappearance" was actually due to the angle at which Galileo was looking. When Earth is in the exact plane of the rings at a certain point in the year, Saturn's rings are hard to see. To Galileo, it looked as though the rings had actually vanished.

After this so-called disappearance, Galileo figured that the planet did not consist of three separate bodies. Rather, Saturn had "handles" protruding from it. This was the only explanation he

Galileo and the Inquisition

During Galileo's lifetime, much of Europe was under the shadow of the oppressive Roman Catholic Church and, especially, the Inquisition. The Inquisition was conducted by a group of people from the church who were charged with the removal of heretics, or people who went against beliefs established by the church. They were then considered criminals, and oftentimes they were punished with horrible cruelty.

A committee of those dedicated to the Inquisition declared that the view that the Sun was the center of the universe, the heliocentric theory, went against the church, saying that it was contrary to what was written in the Holy Bible. The church believed in the geocentric system, a system in which Earth is the center of the universe.

This painting shows Galileo standing before the papal tribunal that conducted the investigation of his scientific beliefs. Galileo was being questioned because he claimed that the Sun was the center of the universe, not Earth. This theory went against the beliefs of the church at the time.

Galileo, who believed in the heliocentric theory because of what his improved telescope allowed him to see, was warned by Cardinal Robert Bellarmine that he should not discuss or teach this theory.

For years, Galileo suppressed his ideas about the heliocentric system. Finally, in 1624, Pope Urban VIII, the leader of the Roman Catholic Church, said that Galileo could write about the heliocentric system as long as he treated it as a mathematical proposition and not a belief.

But Galileo was not able to keep his beliefs under wraps. After publishing his *Dialogue Concerning the Two Chief World Systems*, in 1632, Galileo was called to Rome to face trial before the Inquisition. There, he was found guilty of heresy and was sentenced to house arrest for the rest of his life. In 1642, Galileo died in his house in Florence, still under house arrest and still condemned by the Catholic Church.

In 1659, Christian Huygens *(right)* came up with the theory that Saturn had a system of rings. Gian Domenico Cassini *(left)* discovered in 1675 that there is a gap in Saturn's rings. This gap is now called the Cassini division. An orbiter and a space probe were named after these men.

could think of that could explain the phenomenon. Sadly, Galileo died before ever knowing that he, in fact, was the first person to observe one of the most spectacular sights in our solar system— the rings of Saturn.

Discovering the Rings

For decades, Saturn and its "handles" remained a mystery. In 1659, Dutch astronomer Christian Huygens came up with the theory that Saturn actually had a ring system. By then, a more powerful telescope had been made, one that magnified objects fifty times.

From his observations, Huygens believed Saturn was surrounded by a single ring, which was solid and flat. This theory won over the world of astronomy. Scientists were finally able to identify what they were seeing.

In 1675, using an even more powerful telescope, Italian astronomer Gian Domenico Cassini discovered that Saturn's ring is actually two separate rings made up of thousands of smaller bodies. The space between these rings is called the Cassini division. Both Cassini and Huygens are also credited with the discovery of several of Saturn's moons.

Two

On Saturn

You may think that space travel will someday land a person on Saturn. This, in fact, is physically impossible. Saturn, along with Jupiter, Uranus, and Neptune, are known as the gas giants—planets that are made up almost entirely of gas. There is no actual surface of Saturn, only a gradual change in atmosphere, from loose gases to a molten core.

As the sixth planet from the Sun, Saturn can be viewed best with a small telescope during August and September within the constellation Gemini.

The planet itself was formed more than four billion years ago. The formation of Saturn was much different than that of the terrestrial planets like Earth, planets with solid surfaces and smaller, gaseous atmospheres. Scientists speculate that the gas giants were formed when materials such as rock and ice floating around the solar system were drawn together from the solar cloud. The solar cloud was an immense cloud of hydrogen and helium gas spinning around the universe. The cloud spun at such a rapid pace that it eventually flattened out, much the way a ball of pizza dough becomes flat after a chef spins it in the air.

After the cloud flattened, the gaseous material inside began to solidify into rock and ice. As the bits of rock and ice drew together, the larger pieces fell to the center, creating a "protoplanet," something that would act as the planet's core. Because of where Saturn's protoplanet was located in the original solar cloud, the planet's gravity drew large amounts of gas into itself. This created several gaseous layers that give Saturn a solid look. Eventually, the rocks at the center of the planet melted together to form Saturn's core. Heat remaining from this process may still influence the motion in Saturn's atmosphere.

Saturn's Atmosphere

Since Saturn has a relatively small solid body inside its atmospheric gases, most of the planet can be considered to be atmosphere. Compared to its neighbor Jupiter, Saturn contains much more sulfur, a yellowish nonmetallic element. The presence of sulfur in its atmosphere gives Saturn its yellow hue, making it the golden planet of the universe. But most of Saturn's atmosphere is made up of the elements helium and hydrogen.

Saturn's atmosphere is nearly 91 percent hydrogen—the most hydrogen-rich atmosphere in the solar system. Helium makes up about 3 percent of Saturn's atmosphere. The rest of the atmosphere consists of methane and ammonia.

Saturn's atmosphere is broken into distinct layers. Different parts of Saturn's atmosphere do not mix with each other. Therefore, the layers do not blend with each other, much like how oil and water will separate if allowed to sit.

The outermost layer of the atmosphere, the visible part, is made up of hydrogen and helium gas. Just below the clouds is a layer of thin dust particles with a layer of ammonia ice crystals below that. Below this is a dense layer of ice clouds, mostly consisting of ammonium hydrosulfide. The innermost layer that surrounds the planet's core is mainly water droplets and ice crystals.

Scientists have estimated that Saturn's average temperature hovers around −350°F (−212°C)! To put this into perspective, the

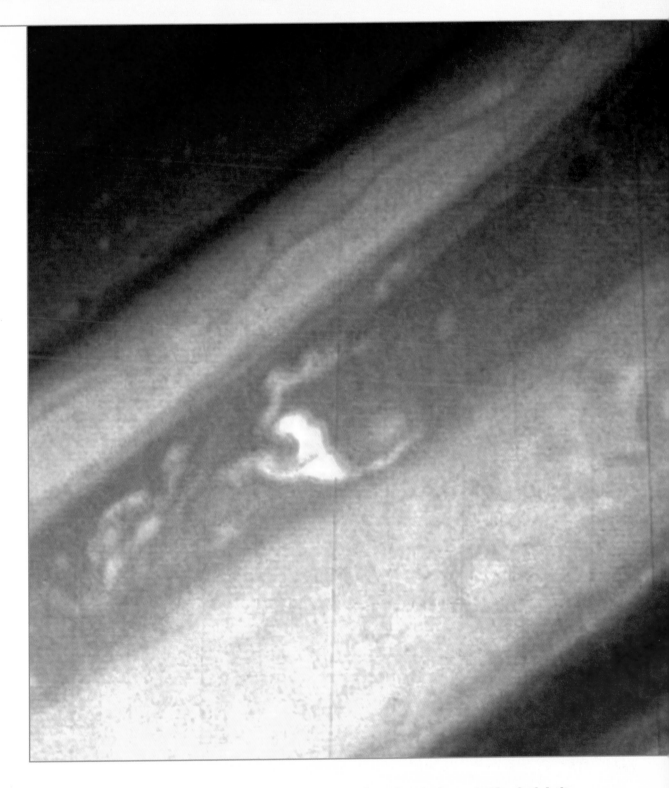

Shown here are examples of clouds in Saturn's northern hemisphere. In the dark belt are small convective clouds. In the lighter zone is another convective cloud with a dark ring. To put this into scale, the smallest features visible in this photograph are 109 miles (175 km) across.

coldest temperature ever recorded on Earth, according to the *Guinness Book of World Records*, was −126.9°F (−88.3°C), which occurred at Vostok, Antarctica, on August 25, 1960.

The surface gravity of the ringed giant is 1.16 times the surface gravity on Earth. So, if you weighed 150 pounds (68 kilograms) on Earth, you would weigh 174 pounds (79 kg) on Saturn.

The mass of Saturn is 5.68×10^{26} kilograms (5.68 with 24 zeros), or ninety-five times greater than the mass of Earth, while its volume is nearly eight hundred times the volume of Earth. Saturn's density, or matter packed into a certain amount of space, is $0.7 \ g/cm^3$ (grams per cubic centimeter), the lowest of any planet in the solar system. In fact, Saturn's density is so low that the planet would actually float in water.

The Magnetosphere

Many planets have a magnetic field, or magnetosphere, surrounding them. A magnetosphere behaves like a giant magnet. On Saturn, the magnetosphere is created by a mantle, or layer, of liquid metallic hydrogen located in the planet's core. The liquid swirls at such a high rate that it generates an electric current and creates the magnetosphere.

The magnetosphere contains many different magnetic currents. It deflects charged particles discharged from the Sun in what is called the solar wind, or the flow of charged particles emitted by the Sun. The particles that make it through the magnetosphere can create many natural phenomena on the planets, such as auroras here on Earth. Auroras are caused when streams of charged particles from the solar wind burst through the magnetosphere, causing the particles to burn up and create an astonishing light show.

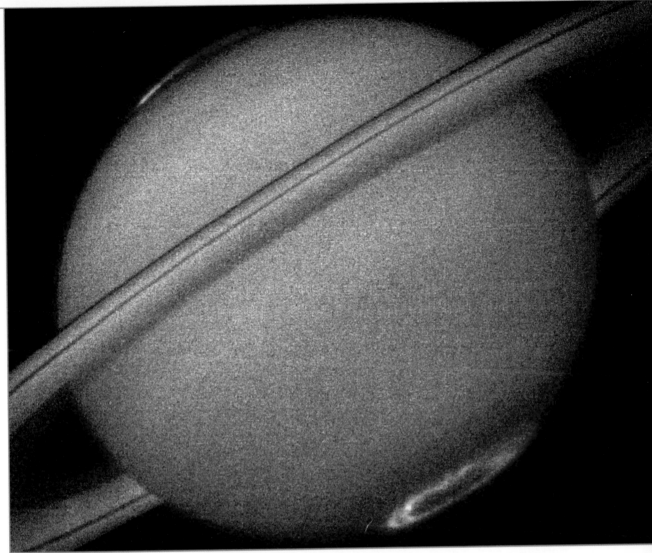

Auroras are displays of light in the upper atmosphere caused by radiation from the Sun interacting with a planet's magnetic field. Shown here are the auroras on Saturn taken by the Hubble Space Telescope in October 1997. Saturn's auroras differ from Earth's. They emit ultraviolet light, which makes them invisible to the human eye. This image was taken by Hubble's spectrograph, which can detect ultraviolet light.

Saturn's magnetosphere is nearly six hundred times stronger than Earth's, yet it is thirty times weaker than Jupiter's. Scientists did not know of Saturn's magnetosphere until the *Pioneer 11* space probe passed near the planet in 1979.

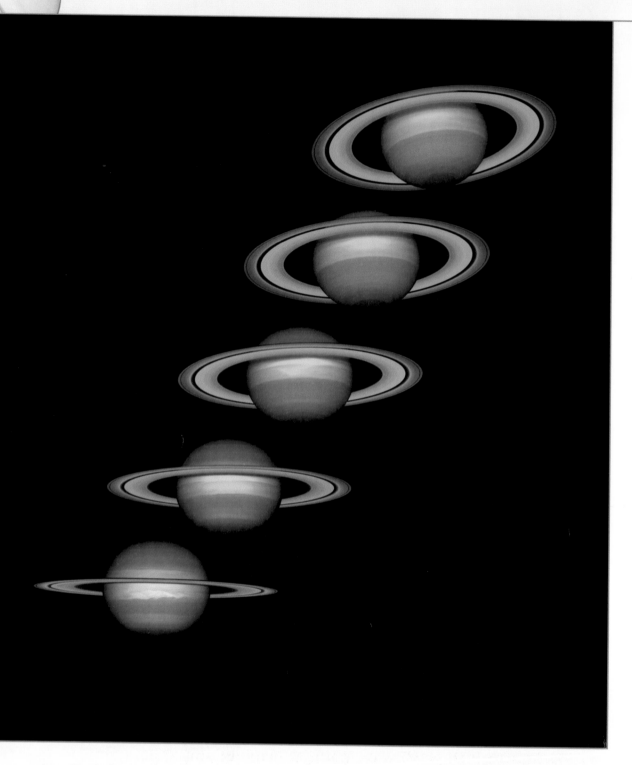

Much like Earth, Saturn's tilt, or the planet's angle on its axis, changes as it moves through its orbit around the Sun. This causes the seasons on Saturn. But it also allows scientists to view Saturn's rings at different angles. Since Saturn's rings are extremely thin, seeing them at a better angle is important to scientists. These five images of Saturn at different angles were taken by the Hubble Space Telescope from 1996 to 2000.

The Winds of Saturn

Wind is a major factor in Saturn's makeup. Wind on Earth is caused in part by the warming of air by the Sun. Being so far from the Sun, Saturn gets as little as 1 percent of the solar energy that Earth receives. Since there is evidence of wind on Saturn—and very strong wind at that—it is believed that the heat creating this wind comes from Saturn itself.

Scientists believe that Saturn's core radiates nearly twice the heat that it absorbs from the Sun. This heat, combined with Saturn's thick, layered atmosphere, causes atmospheric winds to reach speeds as high as 1,100 miles per hour (1,800 km/h). That's more than ten times the strength of a hurricane on Earth.

These winds are another reason humans will never land on Saturn. Suppose Saturn did have a surface like Earth's. The winds are so strong that a large spacecraft such as a space shuttle would be picked up and whisked away like a toy in a tornado.

Saturn is known to have major storms within its atmosphere, though it has far fewer than Jupiter. Much like Jupiter's Great Red Spot, which is actually a giant storm, Saturn is home to a giant white area, which kicks up an enormous and continuous atmospheric storm that rages in the planet's southern hemisphere.

Saturn's Interesting Orbit and Rotation

Saturn's average distance from the Sun is 888.2 million miles (1.42 billion km). Depending on where it is on its orbital path, Saturn can be anywhere between 748 million miles (1.2 billion km) and 1.3 billion miles (2.1 billion km) from Earth. This lengthy orbital path makes Saturn's year 10,804 days long. That means one year on Saturn lasts 29.6 Earth years. On December 31, 2003, Saturn was at its closest point to Earth in thirty years.

Saturn, like the other gas giants, has no set rotation period, or the time it takes for the planet to spin around once. (Earth's rotation period lasts almost twenty-four hours. This is where we get our twenty-four-hour day.)

Since Saturn is not a solid planet such as Earth or Mars, parts of the planet actually rotate at different speeds. Instead of considering the planet body in the rotation, one must consider Saturn's mammoth upper atmosphere in order to trace the planet's variety of rotation periods. Some of these rotation periods make a day on Saturn as short as ten hours and ten minutes or as long as eleven hours and seven minutes. So, Saturn doesn't actually have one time period for its day, like the twenty-four hours we have here on Earth.

Saturn's Dimensions

Saturn is the second largest of all the planets. The equatorial diameter, or the length of a straight line if it ran through the planet's center, is 74,898 miles (120,536 km). That's enormous compared to the smallest planet, Mercury, which is 3,032 miles (4,880 km), and Earth, which is 7,926 miles (12,756 km), about ten times smaller than Saturn.

Of all the planets, Saturn is the most oblate, or flattened at the poles. This appearance is due to Saturn's combination of a speedy rotation and its gaseous makeup. The planet spins at such a rapid rotation—about 6,200 mph (9,975 km/h)—that the gaseous atmosphere at the poles is pressed inward while the atmosphere at the equator bulges outward. This gives Saturn a look similar to that of a deflated basketball on the top and bottom of the planet.

Saturn's Core

Because of Saturn's equatorial bulge, scientists believe that the planet contains a dense inner core of melted rock or a rock-and-ice mixture. This inner core is believed to be ten to fifteen times heavier than Earth's mass.

Saturn's core is surrounded by a mantle of metallic liquid hydrogen, which is then surrounded by ordinary liquid hydrogen. Unfortunately, because of Saturn's dense atmosphere, little else is known about its core. Hopefully, future space expeditions will be able to unravel the mystery of Saturn's core.

Three

The Rings of Saturn

The rings of Saturn are probably the most recognizable and beautiful features in the entire solar system. Other planets such as Jupiter, Uranus, and Neptune possess rings as well, but they are darker and not as distinct as Saturn's glorious rings.

Composition of the Rings

During the seventeenth century, the astronomers who discovered Saturn's rings, and later their characteristics, still believed that the rings were solid. Today, we know that the rings are actually made up of countless particles of ice and rock. These particles are constantly orbiting the main body of the planet.

The size of these orbiting particles varies greatly. While some particles are no larger than grains of sand or small stones, some particles have been measured at nearly a 0.5 mile (0.8 km) across. If all the particles in Saturn's rings were collected into one large mass, it would measure about 60 miles (97 km) across. Though the individual particles in the ring system cannot be detected by telescope, their makeup is known by the scattering of radio signals that are bounced off the particles and returned to spacecraft and satellites.

Each of Saturn's rings has a different name. Shown here in this close-up view taken by the *Voyager 2* spacecraft is the A ring. The gap in the center of the ring is called the Encke division. The small dot at the top left is the shepherding satellite of the F ring called Prometheus (shown in more detail on page 33).

Origin of the Rings

The origin of Saturn's rings is a much-debated mystery of the solar system. Most scientists tend to believe that hundreds of thousands of years ago, an enormous comet hit Saturn's protoplanet. This collision sprayed particles into space that were eventually trapped in an orbit around Saturn. Over time, these larger particles were broken down into smaller and smaller particles, and they began to spread out. The actual ring system was then created when orbiting particles were not able to join together to form a moon. Instead, these particles continued to float around the young planet, trapped in different orbits.

The rings themselves are located in an orbiting area known as the Roche limit. In 1850, French mathematician Edouard Roche proposed the theory that the rings orbit Saturn at such a great speed that no moons would be able to form. Roche said this phenomenon was due to the gravity from orbiting moons that pushes and pulls on objects in space. The Roche limit represents the shortest distance a small satellite can get to a larger satellite before it is torn apart by these gravitational changes.

Over time, the particles located in the rings slammed into each other, breaking apart into smaller particles. Once trapped inside the ring orbit, these particles began to flatten due to the forces created by their orbiting speed. The particles began to spread away from the planet. Eventually, a large series of rings was created. The particles making up the rings would always be trapped in this orbit, unable to spin off into space or crash into the interior of the planet.

Ring particles that are located farther away from the planet move slower than those closer to the planet. The faster-moving particles move toward the planet, while the slower-moving particles get pushed away from the planet. This relationship allows the rings to take on the effect that they are spreading out away from the planet.

Composition of the Ring System

The entire ring system is actually made up of several different smaller ring systems. If looked at from above, the entire ring system has an appearance similar to that of the surface of a music record. Small ring systems are separated by gaps. From images retrieved by the Voyager space missions, nearly one thousand tiny rings can

This image taken by the *Voyager 2* spacecraft shows Saturn's B and C rings. At the top left is the B ring, with the C ring encompassing the rest of the image. Within these rings are more than sixty bright and dark ringlets. This image was made from three separate images taken through ultraviolet, clear, and green filters, so the colors are artificial. The C ring is generally a bland gray, the color of dirty ice.

be detected within the entire ring system. Altogether, the entire ring system measures about 175,000 miles (282,000 km) wide, while the thickness of the rings ranges from 656 feet (200 m) to 9,842 feet (3,000 m).

Saturn's rings are classified using a lettering system. The faint D ring is the closest to Saturn. Its inner edge is about 4,200 miles (6,759 km) away from the outermost part of Saturn's atmosphere. The D ring extends nearly 4,600 miles (7,402 km) outward to the more visible C ring. The C ring then extends about 11,000 miles (17,703 km) away from Saturn. The densest of the rings is the B ring, about 16,000 miles (25,750 km) wide, with its outer edge stopping at the large Cassini division. The division extends for 2,900 miles (4,667 km), separating the B ring from the A ring.

Across the Cassini division from the B ring lies the A ring, measuring nearly 9,100 miles (14,645 km) across. The outermost edge of this ring is nearly 48,000 miles (77,249 km) from the outermost layer of the atmosphere of Saturn. Next to the A ring is the narrow F ring, only 20 to 30 miles (32 to 48 km) across. Beyond the F ring lie the faint G and E rings, both discovered by the *Voyager* spacecraft in the 1970s. The outermost edge of the E ring, the final ring, is about 175,000 miles (282,000 km) from Saturn's outermost atmosphere.

Four

The Moons of Saturn

In 1610, Galileo made an astonishing discovery when he spotted four satellites orbiting Jupiter. Aside from our moon, which has been seen by humans for thousands and thousands of years, Galileo's discovery was the first recorded sighting of moons orbiting other planets.

Then, in 1655, Christian Huygens discovered a large moon orbiting Saturn. This moon would be named Titan, the second-largest moon in the solar system after Jupiter's Ganymede. In 2005, a probe made it past Titan's misty atmosphere and landed on the moon's surface.

Unlike Earth, which has only one moon, Saturn has an extensive system of moons. NASA estimates that Saturn has at least fifty-two moons. The *Cassini* orbiter verified the existence of these moons during its 2004–2008 mission.

The Major Satellites

Much like the planets, Saturn's satellites have been assigned names from Roman mythology. There are seven large satellites, with Titan being the only moon that is the size of a planet.

Titan

As its name suggests, Titan is the largest of all of Saturn's moons. Larger than the planet Mercury, Titan has a diameter

Shown here are layers of haze covering Saturn's moon Titan. This image was taken by the spacecraft *Voyager 1* on November 12, 1980, at a distance of 13,700 miles (22,000 km). The colors are false and are used to show the details of the layers of haze. The upper layer appears orange.

of 3,190 miles (5,134 km). Throughout the entire solar system, only Jupiter's moon Ganymede is larger.

Titan orbits Saturn at a distance of about 760,000 miles (1.2 million km) from the planet's atmospheric surface. In comparison, our moon orbits just an average of 240,000 miles (386,243 km) from Earth.

Titan is believed to be equal parts ice and rock. The rocky core of Titan is surrounded by a surface of ice, with the possibility of a layer of liquid water beneath that.

Unlike other large satellites in the solar system, Titan has one significant characteristic: an atmosphere. Scientists believe Titan's atmosphere exists because extremely cold temperatures surrounding the satellite were not warm enough to burn off the layer of methane, ammonia, and other gases that were trapped in the lunar ices that were released after Titan was formed. Later on, the gases started to escape from the ice, creating the moon's early atmosphere. Much like Earth and Venus, Titan's strong gravity traps these gases and prevents them from escaping into outer space.

Titan's atmosphere is up to 90 percent nitrogen. Other gases include methane, ethane, argon, and hydrogen. This means that Titan and Earth have the only two atmospheres in the solar system that are dominated by nitrogen. Most other atmospheres, like those on Venus and Mars, are mostly carbon dioxide.

Regardless of its atmospheric similarities to Earth, Titan does lack one specific characteristic to make it hospitable for life as we know it: large amounts of oxygen. While no oxygen appears to be in the atmosphere, some scientists believe that oxygen may actually be trapped within the icy surface of the moon.

Mimas

Mimas is the satellite that is closest to Saturn and has a diameter of only 240 miles (386 km) across. Objects have pounded Mimas for thousands of years, giving the moon a heavily cratered surface. One crater in particular, named Herschel, dominates the surface of Mimas. Herschel measures about 60 miles (97 km) across. Scientists believe that the impact that created this crater was about the biggest Mimas could have withstood without the moon shattering into pieces.

Enceladus

Next to Mimas, away from Saturn, is the moon Enceladus. The surface of Enceladus is covered in ice, and its white surface makes

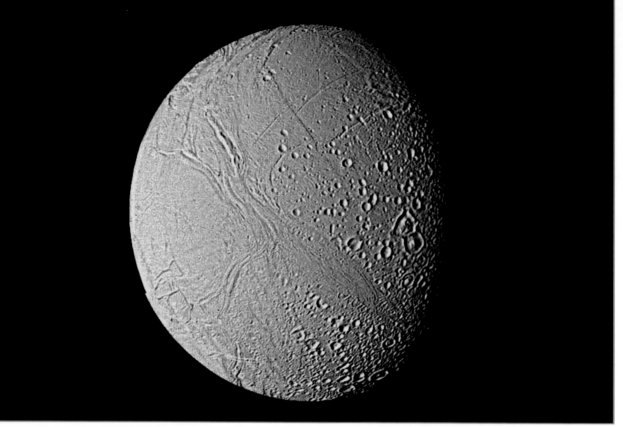

This image of Saturn's moon Enceladus was taken by the *Voyager 2* spacecraft on August 25, 1981, from a distance of 74,000 miles (119,000 km). Enceladus's surface is smooth compared to the other moons. Scientists believe that this smooth surface was caused by cracks in its surface through which water leaked out and poured over craters.

it the most reflective of the Sun's rays of any satellite in the solar system. Enceladus is larger than Mimas and has a relatively smooth, craterless surface. Scientists believe that water from beneath the moon's icy surface may have escaped through cracks in the surface ice and poured over craters, giving Enceladus its smooth appearance.

Tethys

Tethys is the next major satellite next to Enceladus from Saturn. With an icy surface, Tethys has large rifts, or cracks. Scientists believe that this is proof of tectonic activity, or the shifting of large plates below the lunar surface. The largest of these cracks is known as the Ithaca chasm and stretches 60 miles (97 km) wide and more than 2 miles (3.2 km) deep. Tethys also shares its orbit with two other much smaller satellites, one in front and one behind.

Dione

From Tethys, away from Saturn, orbits the similar moon Dione. The surface of Dione is speckled with cratered and noncratered areas, and it has a diameter of 700 miles (1,127 km).

Rhea

The second largest of Saturn's moons is Rhea, with a diameter of 950 miles (1,529 km). Much like the other satellites, Rhea has been resurfaced by icy flows, which have kept down the number of surface cracks.

Shepherd Satellites

While most of Saturn's moons orbit outside the ring system, several minor satellites exist within the ring system itself. These are known as shepherd satellites. Shepherd satellites orbit near the outer edge of a ring system and greatly influence the orbit of the particles within each ring system. The orbits of these satellites cause rifts in the ring system, making gaps appear. These satellites "shepherd," or act as guides to, the particles, keeping the particles within an orbit in the ring system.

Since they travel at much slower speeds near the edge of ring systems, the shepherd satellites attract particles as they go by. These particles slow and fall into an orbit that is closer to the planet, causing the rings to fall in line.

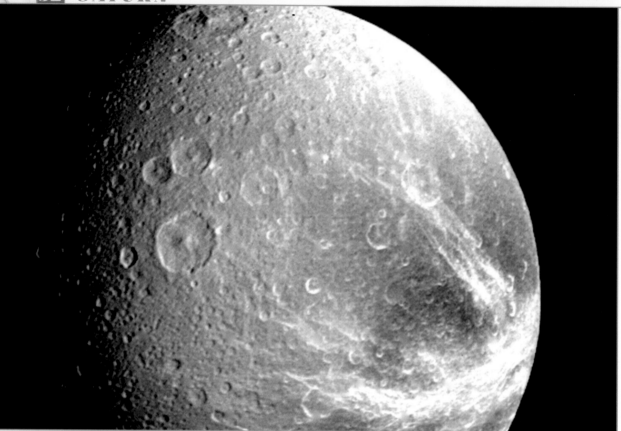

This image of Saturn's moon Dione was taken by the spacecraft *Voyager 1* on November 12, 1980, from a distance of 149,000 miles (240,000 km). The moon's deep impact craters are visible. The streaks at the lower right-hand corner are probably debris that spread out from one of the moon's many impacts with other objects.

Iapetus

Much farther out than Rhea lies Saturn's next moon, Iapetus. With a diameter of 908 miles (1,461 km), Iapetus has one interesting characteristic that makes it different from the other satellites: its southern hemisphere is nearly ten times darker than its northern hemisphere.

When photographed by *Voyager 2* in 1981, Iapetus looked as though its southern hemisphere was disappearing. Scientists believe that this darker appearance may be caused by material from a comet that now covers the satellite's southern hemisphere. Scientists speculate that this material might be organic, which means that it contains carbon and other elements that are the foundations for life.

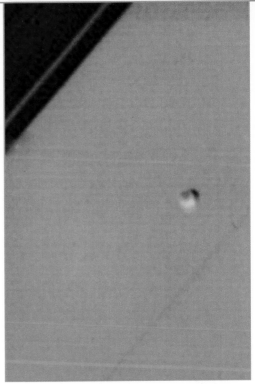

Shown here is the shepherd satellite Prometheus against the background of Saturn. The satellite's brightness suggests that it is made of ice like the larger satellites and ring particles around Saturn. The A ring and Encke division are also visible at the upper left-hand corner. Prometheus is 90 miles (145 km) across.

The Minor Satellites

So far, scientists have been able to identify eleven minor satellites orbiting Saturn. These smaller satellites range in diameter. The largest measures 159 miles (256 km) across, while the smallest measures only 12 miles (19 km) across. These smaller satellites are known as Atlas, Calypso, Epimetheus, Helene, Hyperion, Janus, Pan, Pandora, Phoebe, Prometheus, and Telesto. Many of these satellites have irregular shapes. This is most likely due to the fact that many of these moons were originally parts of other moons, broken off and then trapped in orbits.

Hyperion

The largest of these minor satellites is Hyperion, measuring 159 miles (256 km) across. Scientists believe that Hyperion is a remnant of a larger satellite that was destroyed by the impact of a comet.

Phoebe

Phoebe is the second largest of the minor satellites, measuring 136 miles (219 km) in diameter. Of these minor satellites, Phoebe is the farthest away from Saturn. Phoebe travels in the opposite direction than the other satellites. Much like Iapetus, Phoebe is coated in a dark material, most likely organic.

Janus and Epimetheus

Janus and Epimetheus are known as co-orbiters because they share nearly the same orbit. The two satellites are separated by only 30 miles (48 km). Every four years, the two satellites nearly catch up with each other. Then, instead of colliding, they actually exchange orbits. The outer satellite, which would orbit at a much slower speed, is bumped into the inner orbit and begins to speed up.

Conversely, the inner satellite will jump to the outer orbit and slow down. Scientists believe this interesting relationship points to the possibility that Janus and Epimetheus were in fact one satellite that split into two pieces.

Five

Exploring Saturn, Past and Future

For centuries, man has dreamed of exploring the ringed planet. Over the last three decades, several space programs have neared Saturn and returned dazzling images. Even as you read this, another ambitious satellite is approaching Saturn and will hopefully return images and information that will continue to piece together the mystery of the ringed giant.

Images of Saturn

Exploring Saturn begins with gathering images. But because of particles in Earth's atmosphere, even the most powerful telescopes have trouble seeing objects in deep space. For years, scientists had dreamed of creating and using a space-based observation telescope. But even these telescopes were not able to identify some of Saturn's most distinct features. In fact, before 1980, Saturn was believed to have only eleven moons. At the time of this writing, we know that Saturn has at least thirty-one and maybe even more waiting to be discovered by the Hubble Space Telescope and by the space mission that is expected to reach Saturn in 2004.

The Hubble Space Telescope

Even Galileo's imagination could not have convinced him that one day astronomers would have a permanent space-based

The Hubble Space Telescope was the first space-based telescope. It's better than Earth-based telescopes because it can see space without Earth's atmosphere obstructing the view. The Hubble telescope offers scientists images of space that are clearer and more detailed than those ever taken before. Shown here at the Kennedy Space Center in Florida, the Hubble is being prepared for its launch on the *Discovery* space shuttle mission STS-31 in March 1990.

telescope, capable of seeing into the farthest depths of the universe. And that's exactly what happened when, in 1990, the Hubble Space Telescope was launched. Orbiting at 312 miles (502 km) above Earth's atmosphere, the Hubble telescope is able to avoid the distortions that land-based telescopes have encountered. Over the years, the Hubble telescope has returned stunning images of Saturn. Each image seems to answer age-old questions while revealing even greater mysteries about the ringed giant.

Named after the astronomer Edwin P. Hubble, whose work helped develop theories on the origin of the universe, the Hubble telescope contains a light-gathering mirror 94 inches (240 centimeters) in diameter. This allows the telescope to gather light to produce its phenomenal images of the heavens.

Over the years, the Hubble telescope has returned some astounding images, ones never before imagined. The telescope has detected black holes. It has also captured images of stars that look as though they are giving birth to solar systems, possibly giving us answers to our own origins.

The Hubble telescope is equipped with imagers, which capture images of deep space. It is also equipped with spectrographs, which analyze light. The spectrograph works in many ways like a prism, which breaks down light into its elementary colors. Together, these different colors are called a spectrum. By analyzing the spectrum, scientists are able to figure out the composition of stars and planets.

The Hubble telescope is controlled by radio commands from NASA's Goddard Space Flight Center in Maryland. The telescope is in constant need of updating, so several space shuttle missions have visited it in orbit to add and fix equipment on the precious space telescope.

The *Voyager 1* spacecraft, along with its sister spacecraft, *Voyager 2*, took more than two thousand photos of Saturn and its rings. From these images, scientists learned that Saturn had thousands of little rings instead of the three main rings that were believed to exist. Shown here is *Voyager 1* being launched on September 5, 1977.

Pioneer 11

In September 1979, *Pioneer 11* passed by Saturn at 13,000 miles (20,922 km) from the planet's cloud surface. From there, *Pioneer 11* returned the first up-close images of Saturn and its rings. These stunning images revealed two more moons, as well as another set of rings.

The Voyager Program

In the summer of 1977, NASA launched two spacecraft just sixteen days apart. Known as *Voyager 1* and *Voyager 2*, these two spacecraft traveled nearly one billion miles (1.61 billion km) over three years as they approached the ringed planet. Both craft were about the size of a small car and powered by plutonium, a radioactive substance capable of providing great energy. The spacecraft were the latest technology available to scientists in the late 1970s and were equipped with many scientific devices and several cameras that beamed back images to the headquarters here on Earth.

Since Saturn has no real surface, neither spacecraft was scheduled to land on the planet. They were programmed to simply pass by and return close-up images of Saturn. In November 1980, *Voyager 1* made its initial flyby of Saturn. *Voyager 2*, traveling on a different orbital course, flew by the planet nine months later.

Scientists made astounding discoveries about the gas giant from the images returned by the spacecraft. *Voyager 1* turned up three new moons. From close-up images returned by *Voyager 2*, scientists were able to see that Saturn possesses many more than the three ring systems originally believed to exist. From these images, scientists were able to see that Saturn in fact has thousands of little rings, broken into many ring systems. Together, the *Voyager* craft returned more than two thousand images of Saturn.

Once the *Voyager* spacecraft had returned these images and information about Saturn, their trip was far from over. They just kept going. *Voyager 1* headed in a direction that would one day bring it out of our solar system. Today, it is the farthest spacecraft from Earth. Meanwhile, *Voyager 2* headed to other planets, reaching Uranus in 1986 and Neptune in 1989.

The Cassini-Huygens Mission

On October 15, 1997, NASA launched its most ambitious mission to date: Cassini-Huygens. The *Cassini* orbiter entered Saturn's orbit on June 30, 2004. *Cassini* was scheduled to remain near Saturn for four years, in order to make seventy-four orbits and forty-four close flybys. Much larger than the *Voyager* spacecraft, *Cassini* was also equipped with scientific mapping and data-finding equipment. The orbiter has returned a number of startling images from inside Saturn's ring system and up-close images of the planet itself.

Once *Cassini* approached Saturn in December 2004, a European Space Agency probe named *Huygens* separated from the main orbiter and took a twenty-day journey toward the moon Titan. In January 2005, *Huygens* broke through Titan's atmosphere at

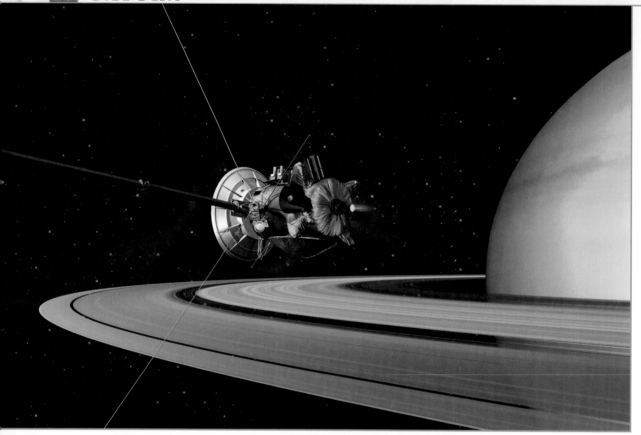

The Cassini-Huygens mission is designed to study Saturn. Shown here is an artist's rendition of *Cassini* during the Saturn orbit insertion (SOI) maneuver. The SOI maneuver will allow the spacecraft to safely fall into Saturn's orbit.

roughly 12,000 mph (19,312 km/h). Parachutes opened, allowing the probe to make a crash landing on the lunar surface.

From Titan, *Huygens* recorded and sent back information about Titan's atmosphere, as well as images from the lunar surface. Because Titan is covered in a dense cloud layer, scientists were not certain what *Huygens* would find once it landed. Since Titan's atmosphere is similar to what Earth's atmosphere was like millions of years ago, scientists entertained the possibility that life existed on this moon.

700 BCE The ancient Assyrians record the first sighting of Saturn.

1610 With his vastly improved telescope, Galileo sees Saturn's rings. He believes Saturn is actually made up of three bodies and later incorrectly concludes that they are handles.

1659 With the aid of a more powerful telescope, Christian Huygens identifies Saturn's rings.

1675 Gian Domenico Cassini discovers Saturn's ring divisions.

1977 NASA launches *Voyager 1* and *Voyager 2*.

1979 Space probe *Pioneer 11* cruises by Saturn, returning the first ever close-up images of the planet and its rings. *Pioneer 11* also reveals two more moons and additional sets of rings.

1980–1981 *Voyager 1* and *Voyager 2* make flybys of Saturn, taking more than two thousand photos of the planet and its rings. From these images, scientists learn that Saturn has thousands of rings.

1990 The Hubble Space Telescope is launched by the United States.

1997 NASA launches the Cassini-Huygens mission.

2004 The *Cassini* and *Huygens* spacecraft fly near Saturn and returns images from inside Saturn's ring system.

2005 *Huygens*, a probe, lands on the surface of Titan. It records and sends back to *Cassini* information about Titan's atmosphere, as well as images from its surface.

2006 *Cassini* records a hurricane-like storm at the south pole of Saturn. The storm was about 5,000 miles (8,046 km) across—nearly two-thirds the diameter of Earth.

2007 *Cassini* captures a six-sided hexagonal feature on Saturn's north pole. The honeycomb-shaped vortex measures roughly 15,000 miles (26,000 km) across.

Glossary

ammonia A colorless gas that has a very strong smell.

density The mass per unit of volume of a substance.

diameter The distance of a straight line through the center of a body.

equatorial Relating to the equator, or the imaginary circle around a body that is of equal distance to each pole.

geocentric Having Earth as the center of the universe.

gravity The force each body in the universe exerts on every other body.

heliocentric Having the Sun as the center of the universe.

helium A lightweight, colorless, nonflammable gas.

hydrogen A colorless, odorless, highly flammable gas.

magnetosphere The space around a celestial body that is dominated by its magnetic field.

mass The measure of the amount of matter, or the material substance that occupies space, in an object.

methane A colorless, odorless, flammable gas that is sometimes used as fuel.

molten Made liquid by heat.

oblate Flattened at the poles.

organic Of or derived from living organisms; concerned with carbon compounds of living things.

radiate To spread out from a center.

rotation The spinning motion of a celestial body on its axis.

sulfur A pale yellow nonmetallic element.

telescope An instrument used to magnify objects for a clearer view.

For More Information

Kennedy Space Center
Spaceport U.S.A.
Kennedy Space Center, FL 32899-0001
(321) 452-2121
Web site: http://www.ksc.nasa.gov
NASA's space vehicle launch facility.

National Aeronautics and Space Administration (NASA)
300 E Street SW
Washington, DC 20546
E-mail: comments@hq.nasa.gov
Web site: http://www.nasa.gov
An agency of the United States government responsible for the nation's space
program.

National Air and Space Museum
Smithsonian Institution
Washington, DC 20560-0321
Web site: http://www.nasm.si.edu
The largest collection of historic air and spacecraft in the world.

Web Sites

Due to the changing nature of Internet links, Rosen Publishing has
developed an online list of Web sites related to the subject of this
book. This site is updated regularly. Please use this link to access
the list:

http://www.rosenlinks.com/lnp/satu

For Further Reading

Faradon, John. *1,000 Facts of Space*. Essex, UK: Miles Kennedy Publishing, 2001.

Landau, Elaine. *Saturn* (Watts Library: Space). London, UK: Franklin Watts, 2000.

Paschoff, Jay M. *Stars and Planets: A Peterson Field Guide*. New York, NY: Houghton Mifflin, 2000.

Shea, William, and Mariano Artigus. *Galileo in Rome*. New York, NY: Oxford University Press, 2003.

Walters, Thomas R. *Smithsonian Guide to the Planets*. New York, NY: Macmillan, 1995.

Bibliography

Asimov, Isaac. *Frontiers: New Discoveries About Man and His Planet, Outer Space, and the Universe.* New York, NY: Dutton, 1989.

Davis, Kenneth. *Don't Know Much About the Universe.* New York, NY: Perennial, 2001.

Faradon, John. *1,000 Facts of Space.* Essex, UK: Miles Kennedy Publishing, 2001.

Gehrels, Tom, and Mildred Shapley Matthews, eds. *Saturn.* Tucson, AZ: University of Arizona Press, 1984.

Macy, Samuel. *Patriarchs of Time.* Athens, GA: The University of Georgia Press, 1987.

Walters, Thomas R. *Smithsonian Guide to the Planets.* New York, NY: Macmillan, 1995.

Washburn, Mark. *Distant Encounters: The Exploration of Jupiter and Saturn.* New York, NY: Harcourt Brace Jovanovich, 1983.

Index

About the Author

Charles Hofer is an editor and writer living in New York City.

Credits

Cover © Corbis; pp. 4–5, 9, 15, 23, 25, 28, 30, 32, 40 © NASA/ Jet Propulsion Laboratory/CalTech; p. 6 © Araldo de Luca/Corbis; p. 8 © Gustavo Tomsich/Corbis; p. 10 © Hulton Archive/Getty Images, Inc.; p. 11 © Science Photo Library; p. 17 © J. T. Trauger (Jet Propulsion Laboratory)/NASA; p. 18 © NASA/Hubble Heritage Team; p. 33 © Goddard Space Flight Center/NASA; p. 36 © Kennedy Space Center/NASA; p. 38 © Marshall Space Flight Center/NASA.

Designer: Tom Forget; Editor: Beth Bryan